Science for All

Book 1

For Class 1

AF587510

For CBSE Schools

Based on CCE

Ruchi Arora

Pegasus

Preface

Science today has ceased to be just a subject which is limited to books only. It has become a way of life. In every walk of life we require science; we need it to drive a car, watch television, click a photograph or even when light up our room! Science is actually knowledge that pervades nature on the whole.

Every child is a scientist in their own way as they are always full of curiosity and are always ready to explore new areas of life. It is a must that we elders keep this spirit of questioning alive and active.

Keeping this in mind and to inculcate a deep interest and insight into this very subject have we conceived our series Science for All. It is a graded series for the primary section enriched with texts that give profound knowledge to the young learners in a simple child-friendly way. The series has been authored by a senior teacher who has and is still dedicating her years teaching Science in a much reputed school of Delhi.

The books contain questions of all types, subjective and objective both. Each chapter has a section of activities at the end. The activities are varied ranging from drawing, colouring, pasting pictures to group activities and pair and share. Along with recapitulation of the text, the children learn to research and co-operate with others through these activities.

The books are full of colourful illustrations and photographs which help the children understand better.

From the Author

Science has become a way of life today whether one has to connect to the world by using the internet or light a bulb. Our day to day activities are governed by the principles of science knowingly or unknowingly. Scientific bent of mind is a judicious way to deal with the small obstacles that governs our everyday life.

The series **Science for All** is prepared in accordance with the new syllabus prescribed by NCERT on the basis of CCE (Continuous and Comprehensive Evaluation). CCE emphasizes on the continuous learning by different methods to develop creativity, reasoning, analytical and thinking abilities in the learner.

In this series, we have emphasized on the learning of science through simple activities and observations. The books are related to the immediate environment of a child and explain everything that he sees in the light of scientific knowledge. This will facilitate better understanding of the facts of science. The books are written in simple and child friendly language with lots of illustrations and activities that the child will enjoy doing. This will enhance the participation of the learners; in other words encourage 'learning by doing'. It will stimulate the learner's thinking and scientific temper and encourage the overall development and holistic personality of the child.

The exercises given at the end of each lesson contains the questions of both types as per CCE norms, i.e. related to Formative Assessment and Summative Assessment. This will make their concept more clear and inspire them to apply their knowledge every moment. The group activities will enhance group learning and social interaction of the child.

Ruchi Arora

Contents

Unit 1 We and Our Surrounding

Unit 2 Plant Life

Unit 3 Animal Life

Unit 4 Human Body

Unit 5 Our Universe

UNIT 1 We and Our Surroundings

1 Myself

1. My name is ____________________.
2. I am a ____________________.
3. I am ______________ years old.
4. I study in ______________class.
5. I study in ______________________ school.
6. My father's name is ____________________.
7. My mother's name is ____________________.

8. I have __________ brother / sister.
9. I live in ____________________ .
10. The colour I like most is ____________________.
11. The fruit I like most is ____________________.
12. The vegetable I like most is ____________________ .

Paste your recent photograph.

This is me.

Paste or draw the picture of your favourite fruit.

__________ is my favourite fruit.

Draw or paste the picture of your favourite game.

__________ is my favourite game.

Do you play in the park every evening? Draw a park scene and colour it.

A. Colour the box with the correct option for yourself.

1. I am tall ☐ short ☐
2. I am fat ☐ thin ☐
3. I am dark ☐ fair ☐
4. I have short ☐ long ☐ hair.
5. I have black ☐ , blue ☐ , brown ☐ eyes.

2 Our Beautiful World

Our world is a beautiful place. All things that we see around us form the world.

1. It has the sun, the moon and many stars.

Moon and stars   Sun

2. It has rivers and mountains.

River   Mountains

3. It has different kinds of plants, animals and birds.

Trees   Lion   Cat   Birds

4. It has different types of houses and buildings.

Multi storied   Pucca house   Kuchha house

5. It has different types of people who wear different types of clothes and eat different types of food.

Clothes   Foods

6. It has different types of vehicles.

Helicopter   Aeroplane

Bus   Truck   Bicycle   Scooter   Train

The world has many more things. Our world is wonderful.

A. **Look at the following pictures and write (A) for animals and (B) for birds.**

B. **Match these things with the place where they are found.**

C. Aman has seen the two pictures given below. He is confused. Help him find which picture shows daytime and which one shows night. Colour them too.

3 Living and Non-Living Things

Our world is full of different types of things. It has both living things and non-living things.

Living things

The plants, animals and human beings are living things.

Cow

Plant

Living things grow.

Living thing eat.

Living things breathe.

Living things move.

Living things reproduce.

Living things feel.

Non-living things

Non-living things are those which do not breathe, do not grow, do not reproduce and do not move. Things like tables, chairs, fans, toys etc are all non-living things. Non-living things can be natural or man made.

Natural things

Things that are found in nature are called natural things. These are not made by man. Some natural things that we find around us are rocks, water, mountains, trees and the sky.

Man-made things

Things made by man are called man-made things. Non-living things like pen, paper, table, chair, clothes etc are all man made things.

Paper and Pen

Table

Clothes

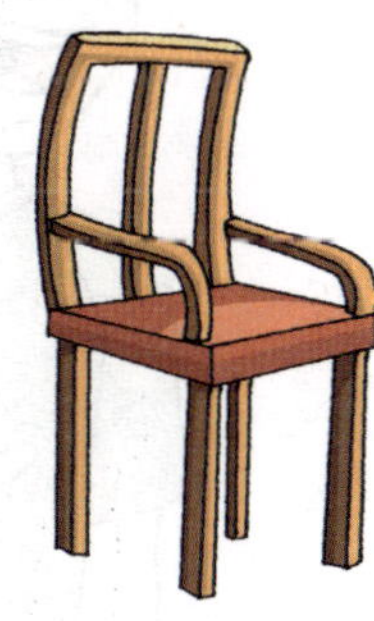

Chair

A. Look at the given pictures and write (L) for living thing and (N) for non-living.

B. Circle the odd one out.

Table	Chair	Parrot	Pen
Elephant	Giraffe	Lion	House
Tree	Rock	Sea	Hill
Goat	Water	Duck	Boy

C. The following things are telling about themselves. Tick them (✓) if they are right and cross (X) them if they are wrong.

D. Colour the living things in the pictures given below.

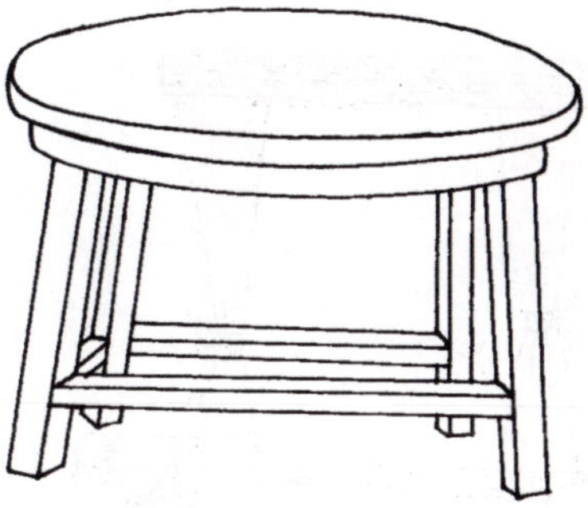

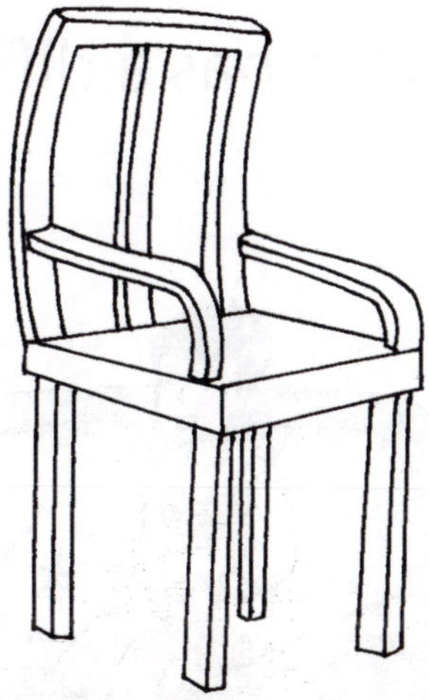

Activity time

Collect pictures of living and non-living things and paste them in a scrapbook and write the name of each.

4 Our House

A house is a place where we all live in. Our house protects us from heat, cold, rain and the wind. It keeps us safe from thieves and animals too.

Rooms in a house

We live in a house with our family. A house has many rooms. Each room has a different use.

It has drawing room to receive guests.

It has a dining room to eat food.

It has a bedroom to take rest and to sleep.

It has a study room to read and study.

It has bathrooms to take bath.

It has a kitchen where food is cooked.

A house is where we rest and spent time with our families. We keep all our belongings in our house. We all love our houses.

Do yourself

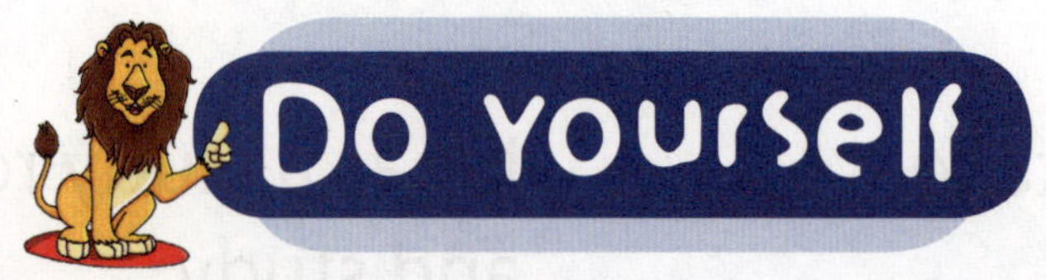

A. Match the given objects to the places where they are found.

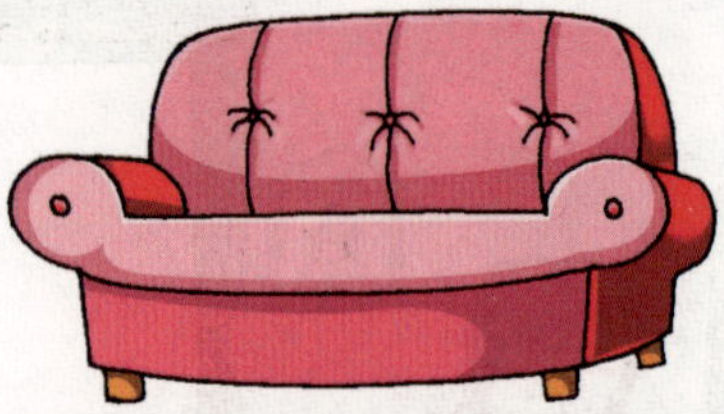

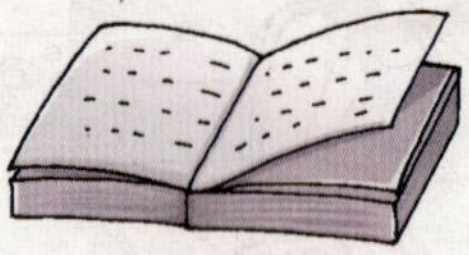

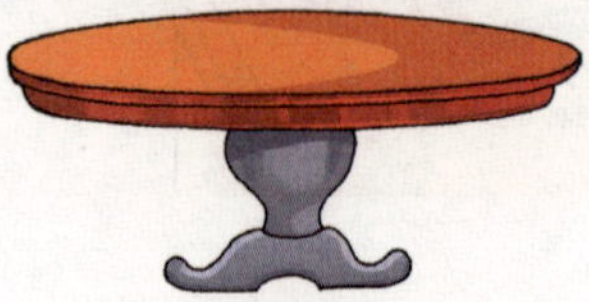

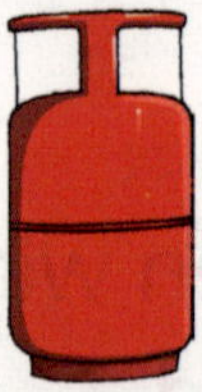

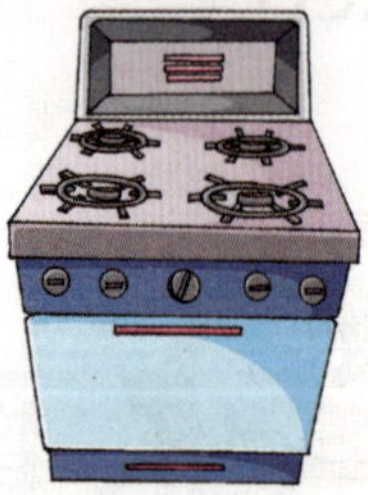

Dining room

Bedroom

Kitchen

Bathroom

Study room

Drawing room

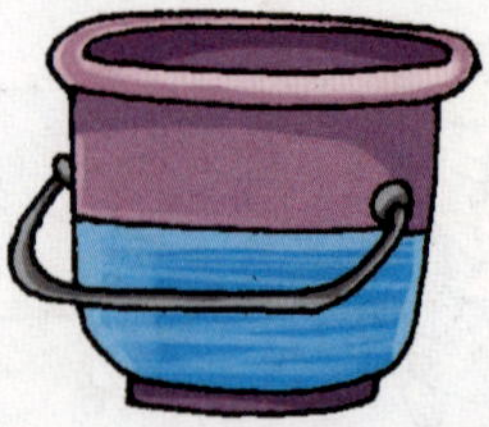

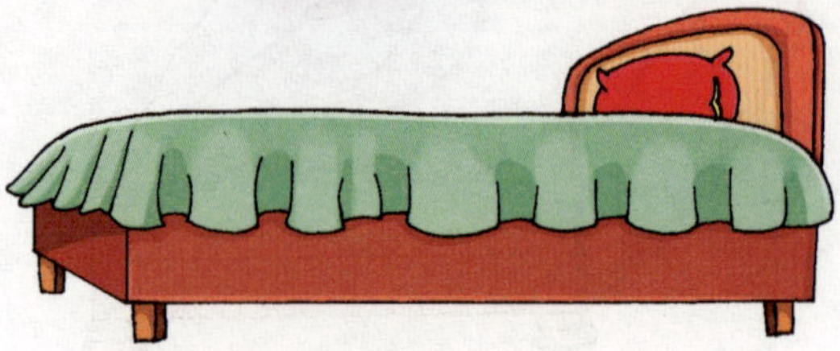

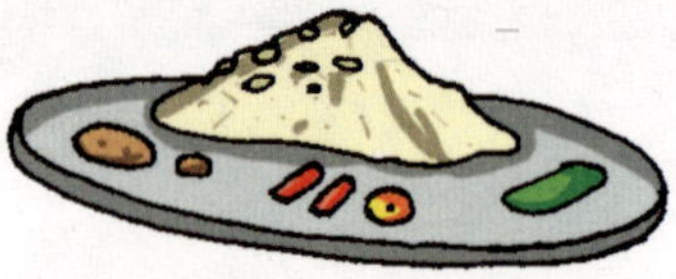

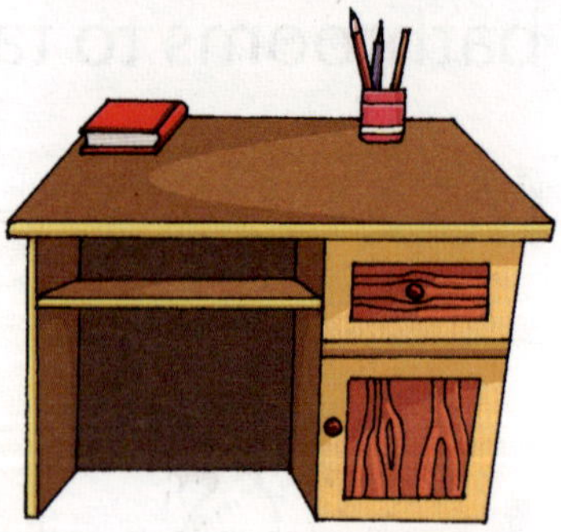

B. Solve the cross word puzzle with the help of picture clues.

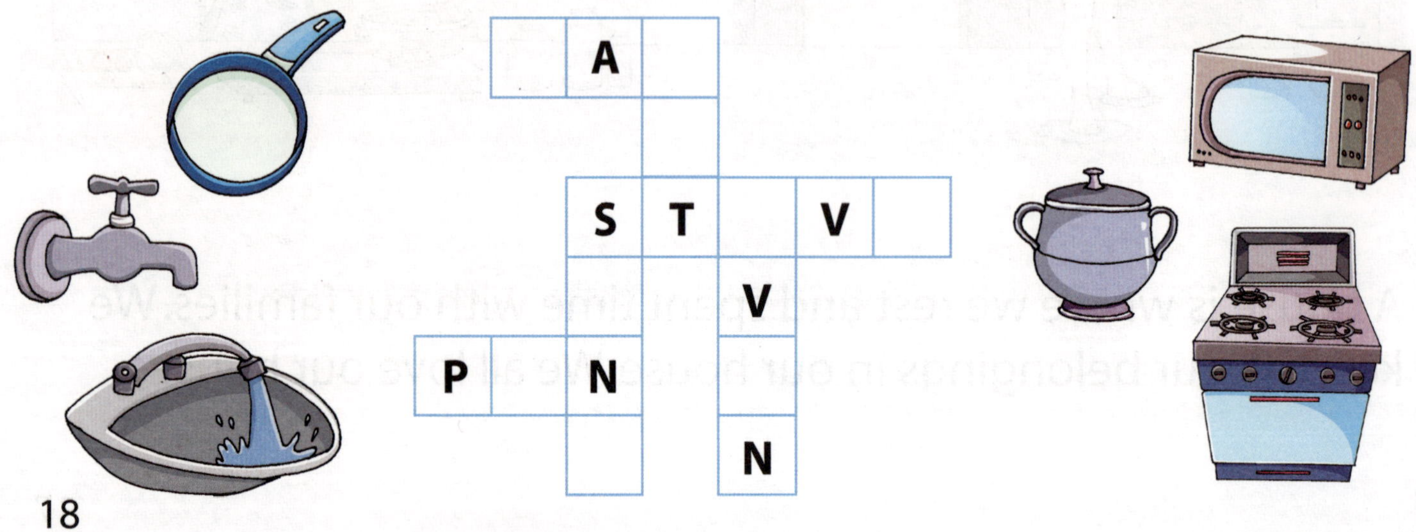

C. Answer the following questions.

1. Why do we need a house?

   ____

2. Where does your mother cook food in the house?

   ____

3. Where do you sleep in the house?

   ____

D. Name any two things that you can find in the given rooms.

a. Drawing room ____________ ____________

b. Kitchen ____________ ____________

c. Bedroom ____________ ____________

d. Bathroom ____________ ____________

E. Match the following

A	B
Receive guests	Kitchen
Study	Bedroom
Cook	Drawing room
Eat	Bathroom
Sleep	Study room
Take bath	Dining room

Activity time

The squirrel has lost his way. Help him find his way home.

5 Safety Rules

Safety means staying away from harm. We should follow some simple rules to keep ourselves safe. These are called **safety rules.**

Safety at home

1. Never play with sharp objects like blade, knife and scissors.
2. Never play with switches and plugs.
3. Keep away from medicines.
4. Always tell your parents where you are playing.
5. Never play with matches or lighters. You may burn yourself.

Safety at school

1. Always walk in a queue in the stairs. Never rush or push while going down the stairs.
2. While playing, do not push or pull anyone. Somebody may get hurt if you do so.

3. Do not play in the class. Always play in the school playground.
4. Do not throw duster, chalk pieces and other things at one another.

Safety while travelling

1. Do not get in or get down from a moving bus or car. It may hurt you.
2. Stand in a queue to get into a bus.
3. Do not put your head or your hand out of the window of a moving bus or car.
4. Do not stand on the foot board of a moving bus. Do not throw things out of a moving vehicle. It may hurt someone.

Safety on roads

1. Always walk on the footpath.
2. Obey all the traffic rules.
3. Always use the zebra crossing or the subway to cross the road.

4. Never play on or near the road.
5. Never take lift from a stranger. It can be dangerous.

Safety while playing

1. Never play on the road. It is safe to play in a park.
2. Do not go alone for swimming. Always go with an adult.

3. Do not pluck flowers or leaves from plants. They may harm you.

4. Do not tease or hurt animals. They may bite you.

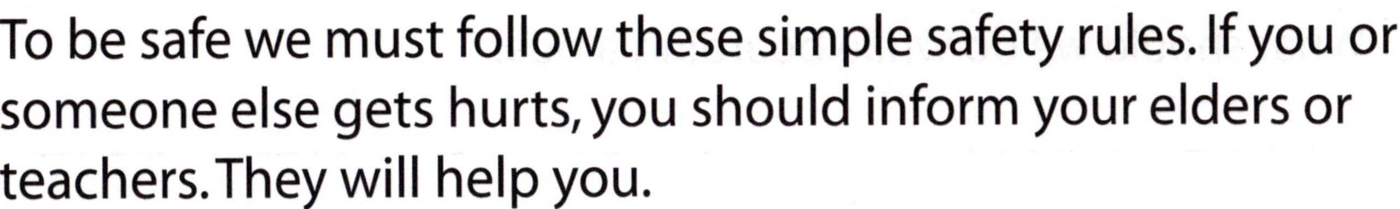

To be safe we must follow these simple safety rules. If you or someone else gets hurts, you should inform your elders or teachers. They will help you.

A. Fill in the blanks with the correct word from the brackets.

1. Always walk on ______________. (road / footpath)
2. ______________ go alone for swimming. (do / do not)
3. Do not play with ______________. (fire / toys)
4. Always make a ______________ to get in the bus. (queue/ crowd)

B. Tick (✓) the correct picture and cross (X) the worng picture.

C. Answer the following questions.

1. Why should we follow safety rules?

____

2. What should we do while boarding a bus?

____

3. Write any two safety rules that should be followed in school.

____

4. What should we do if someone gets hurt?

____

D. Tick (✓) the correct statement and cross (X) out the wrong one.

1. Never play on busy road. ☐
2. Always keep away from medicine. ☐
3. Play with blades, knives and scissors. ☐
4. Put your hands out of a moving bus. ☐
5. Use zebra crossing to cross the road. ☐

Activity time

- Make a chart on '**Safety Rules at Home**' and paste it in your room.
- Make a chart on '**Safety Rules at School**' and paste it in your classroom.

6 Our Helpers

Many people help us in our day to day life. They are our helpers. These are the people who work for us. Different people do different work.

Farmer  A farmer grows food grains for us.

Teacher  A teacher teaches us in school.

Doctor  A doctor treats sick people.

A policeman  A policeman catches thieves.

Postman  A postman brings letters for us.

Carpenter  A carpenter makes furniture for us.

Plumber  A plumber repairs water taps.

Electrician  An electrician repairs electrical gadgets.

Tailor  A tailor stitches clothes for us.

Cobbler  A cobbler repairs our shoes.

Chemist  A chemist sells medicines.

Mason  A mason makes houses for us.

Sweeper  A sweeper keeps our streets clean.

Greengrocer  A greengrocer sells vegetables.

A. Fill in the blanks with the right option.

1. ________________ grows food grains. (plumber/farmer)
2. ________________ sells medicines. (chemist/doctor)
3. ________________ teaches us in school. (postman/teacher)
4. ________________ repairs electrical gadgets. (electrician/carpenter)
5. ________________ stitches clothes for us. (tailor/cobbler)

B. Answer the following questions.

1. Who brings letters for us?

   ____

2. Who catches thieves?

   ____

3. Who cures you when you fall sick?

   ____

4. Who makes the house for us?

   ____

C. **The names of four helpers are hidden in the word search puzzle given below. Circle them.**

J	T	E	A	C	H	E	R
S	G	E	H	H	N	R	O
K	K	L	C	E	S	D	S
R	P	E	N	M	E	R	L
K	G	T	A	I	L	O	R
B	N	W	T	S	L	I	R
M	E	R	D	T	G	X	S
S	A	I	Z	X	J	P	O
L	T	C	N	O	T	V	S
D	O	C	T	O	R	S	D

D. **The pictures of some animals carrying balloons with a letter written on it are given below. Arrange these letters and see what word you get.**

E. Circle the odd one out.

1. A doctor needs

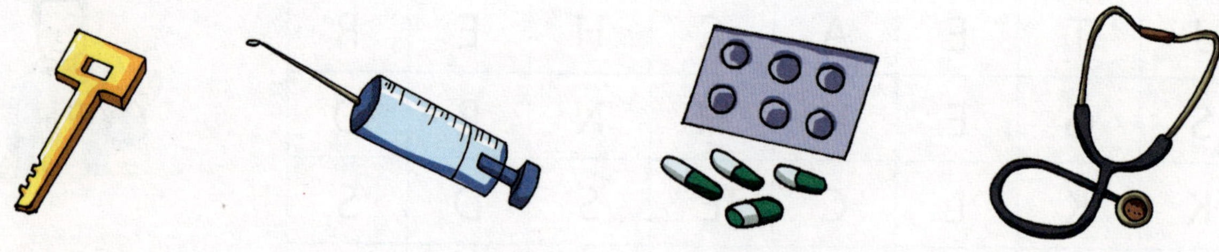

2. A farmer needs

3. A teacher needs

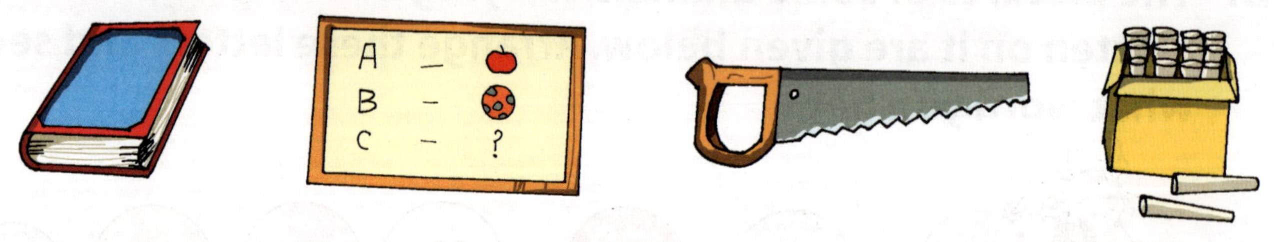

4. A tailor needs

F. Unscramble the given occupations. Use the picture clues to do so.

1. OCTDRO ____________________

2. TSOMPAN ____________________

3. IAOLTR ____________________

4. AFRREM ____________________

5. ECATERH ____________________

6. NSAOM ____________________

G. Alice has gone to the market with a lot of work. Help her by telling her where to go.

a. Alice is sick

____

b. Wants to stitch a frock

____

c. Wants to mend her shoes

____

Activity time

There must be many people in your neighbourhood who help you in your day to day life. With the help of your parents, try to find out their names. Write their name and occupation in your notebook.

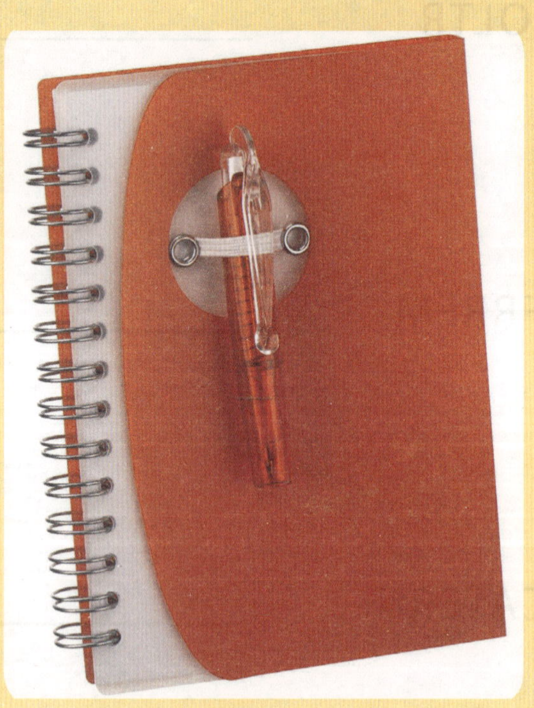

7 Our Neighbourhood

The area around our house is our neighbourhood. We see many things in our neighbourhood. We see people, animals and plants. We also see buildings, shops and vehicles.

We must keep our neighbourhood clean.

We may fall ill if it is dirty. We should grow more plants and trees. It will make our neighbourhood clean and green. A clean and green neighbourhood helps us to stay healthy.

Here are some important places of our neighbourhood.

Park

School

Police Station

Post Office

Bank

Market

Hospital

Bus Stop

Metro Station

A. Look at the picture given below and discuss with your teacher what all you can see in the picture.

B. You have seen many shops in your neighbourhood. Match the given items with the shops where you can find these items.

	Book shop
	Bakery
	Chemist
	Toy shop
	Greengrocer

C. Answer the following questions.

1. What is the area around your house called?

 ____

2. Name any two important places of your neighbourhood.

 ____

3. You are going for a picnic with your parents. Your mother gives you a banana to eat. What will you do with the peel of the banana?

 ____

D. Look at the pictures given below. Tick (✓) the things that you will find in your neighbourhood.

Always remember

Do not litter the neighbourhood.

Throw the waste into a dustbin.

Grow more trees and plants.

Activity time

Go to a nearby shop in your neighbourhood. It can be a stationary shop or a grocery shop. Write the names of any five things you get in that shop. Paste the wrappers of the things in your scrapbook if possible.

8 Plants Our Friends

We see plants all around us. Plants are our friends. Let us have a look at the different parts of a plant.

Parts of a plant

A plant has different parts. It has roots, stem, branches, leaves, flowers and fruits.

Root: Roots are inside the soil. They hold the plant in the soil.

Stem: Stems hold plants upright and straight. It takes food and water to all parts of the plant.

Leaf: Plants have many leaves. Leaves make food for the plant. Some plants have big leaves and some have small leaves

Flowers and fruits: Most plants bear flowers. Flower is the beautiful part of a plant. Fruits are those parts of the plant which we can eat. Many fruits have seeds inside them.

Seed: A seed has a baby plant inside it. Most plants grow from seeds.

Vegetables

A Plant with Flowers

Fruits

We get many things from plants. Plants give us fruits, vegetables, flowers and many more things. We must take care of plants. We should plant more trees. We must not cut trees. We should not pluck flowers.

A. Answer the following questions.

1. Which part of the plant is under the soil?

   ____

2. What is the work of a leaf?

   ____

3. What is the work of a stem?

   ____

4. Which part of a plant has seeds inside?

   ____

5. Why is seed important to us?

   ____

6. Why should we not cut trees?

   ____

B. Label the parts of the plant in the given picture.

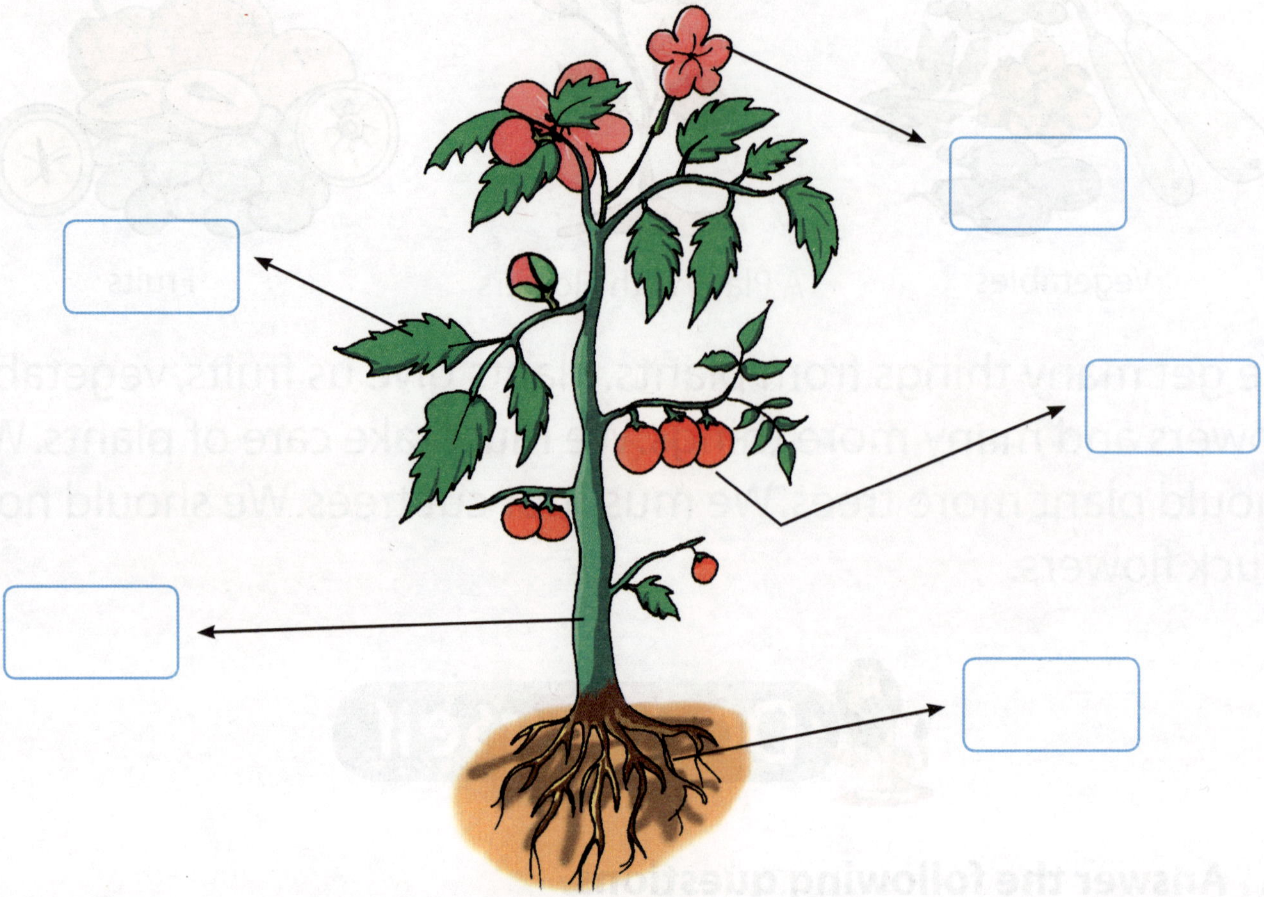

C. Chimpu monkey is throwing mangoes from the tree. Help Della to find the right mango to place in the given blanks.

(Clue: Read the words written on the mango)

1. The ___________ prepares food for the plant.
2. The ________ absorbs water and mineral from the soil.
3. Fruits have ___________ inside them.
4. The __________ helps the plant to stand straight.

D. Some letters are given in the tree below. Using those letters write the names of the parts of a plant. You can use each letter more than once.

Activity time

- Go to the nearby park along with your parents. Take the sample of different types of leaves and flowers. Paste them in your scrapbook. (Do not pluck the flowers and leaves but take only fallen leaves and flowers.)
- Draw a tree on a drawing sheet. Colour the stem brown and leaves green with thumb painting.

9 Plants as Food

Plants are very important for us. We get many useful things from plants. Plants give us fruits and vegetables.

Fruits

Vegetables

Plants gives us cereals and pulses too.

Rice

Wheat

Corn

Wheat, rice, corn and barley are cereals.

All dals, grams, peas, kidney beans are pulses.

Pulses

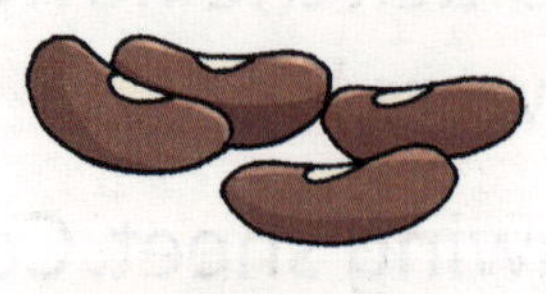

Kidney Beans

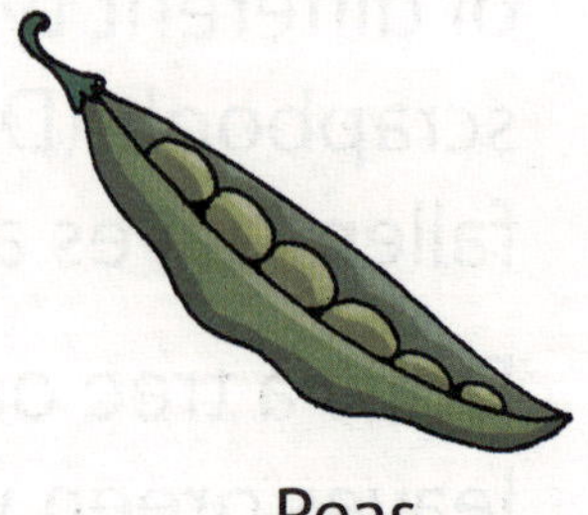

Peas

We get tea, coffee, sugar from plants.

Coffee beans

Sugar

Tea

We get many more things from plants like oil, medicine and wood.

Wood

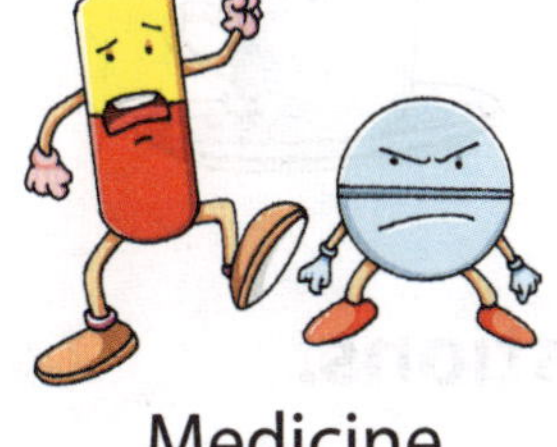
Medicine

Oil

A. Identify the given pictures and write their names. The first letter is given to you.

O ____________

B ____________

P ____________

P ____________

C ____________

G ____________

B. Write (P) in the given box for the things we get from plants and (A) for the things we get from animals.

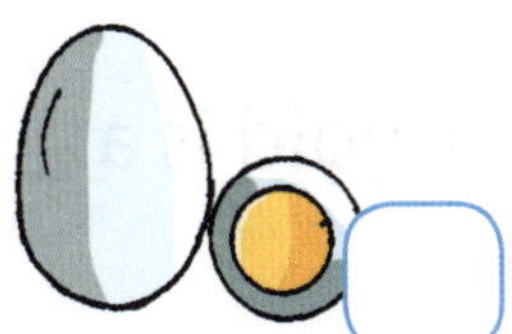

C. Answer the given questions.

1. Why are plants useful to us?

____

2. Write the name of any two fruits you like.

______________ ______________

3. Write the name of any two vegetables you like to eat.

______________ ______________

4. Write any four things we get from plants.

________ ________ ________ ________

D. Fill in the blanks.

1. Potato is a ____________. (fruit / vegetable)
2. ____________ is a fruit. (apple / onion)
3. Wheat and rice are known as ____________. (pulses / cereals)
4. We get wood from ____________. (trees / animal)
5. Marigold is a ____________. (fruit / flower)

E. Circle the names of the food items in the word search puzzle. Use the picture clues to do so.

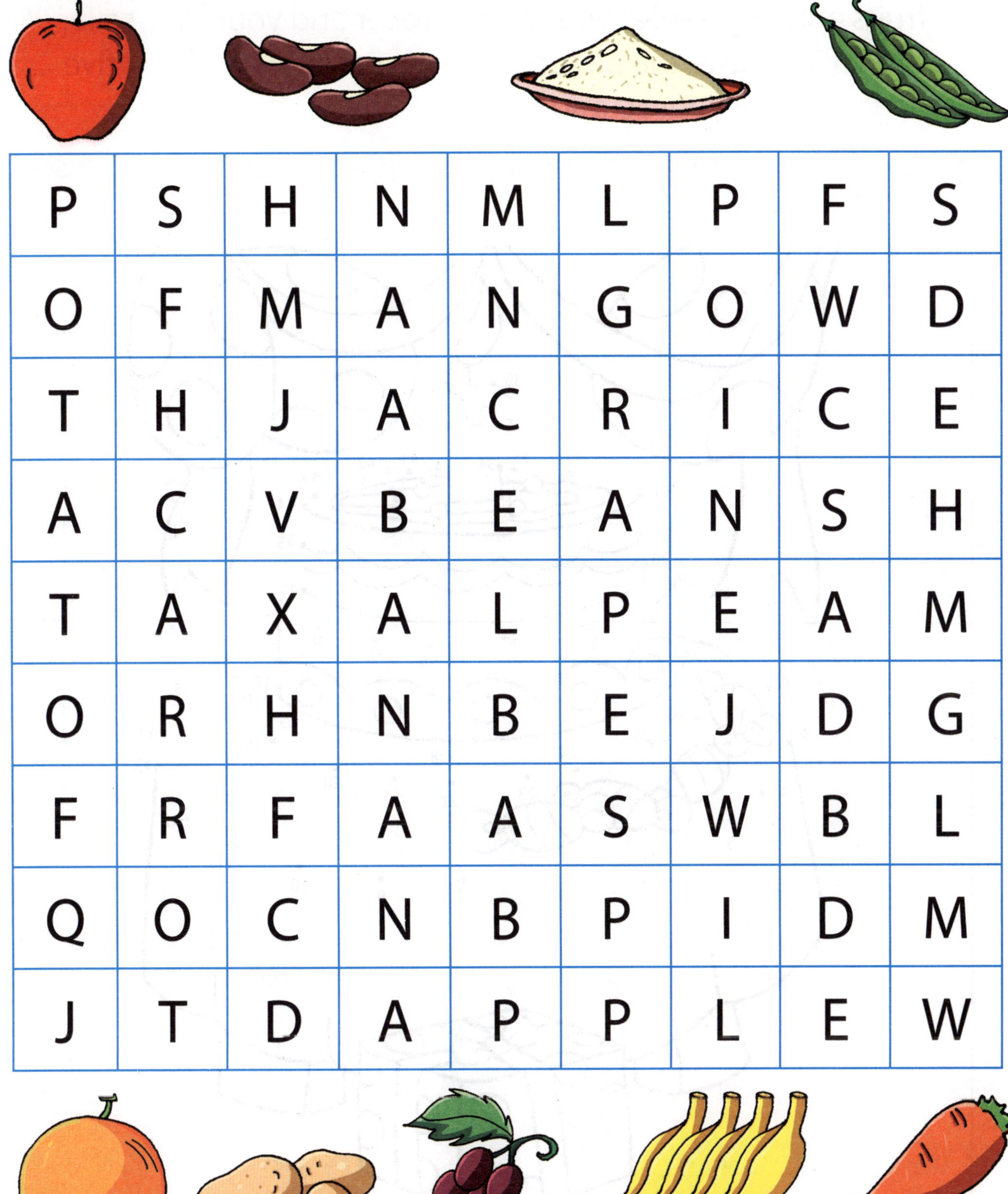

P	S	H	N	M	L	P	F	S
O	F	M	A	N	G	O	W	D
T	H	J	A	C	R	I	C	E
A	C	V	B	E	A	N	S	H
T	A	X	A	L	P	E	A	M
O	R	H	N	B	E	J	D	G
F	R	F	A	A	S	W	B	L
Q	O	C	N	B	P	I	D	M
J	T	D	A	P	P	L	E	W

Activity time

- Go to the market with your parents. Find out which seasonal fruits and vegetables your greengrocer and your fruit-seller are selling. Paste the pictures of five seasonal fruits and five vegetables in your scrapbook.
- Complete the given picture by joining the dots. Colour it also.

10 Animals Our Friends

There are many kinds of animals in the world. We see many of them around us. Some are big and some are small.

Tiger Wolf Lion Giraffe

Lions, tigers, giraffes, elephants, bears and rhinoceroses are some of the bigger animals. Most of these animals have four legs. They live in jungles. We can see them in the zoo also.

Dogs, cats, rats, birds, insects and worms are some small animals. We see most of these around our house or in the zoo.

Bird

Ladybird

Cat

Dog

Birds

Birds are important members of the animal kingdom. There are many kinds of birds. Most of them can fly. Birds have wings which help them to fly.

Duck

Some birds such as ostrich, emu, penguin cannot fly. They can only walk and run.

Some birds like duck, crane can swim. Birds have no teeth. They eat with their beaks. Most birds make nests to live in.

Ostrich Penguin

Insects

Insects are small animals with more than two legs. They have wings to fly. Most insects have six legs.

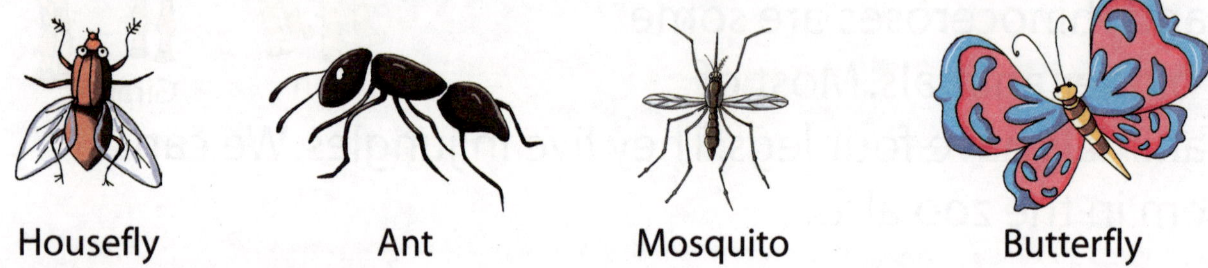

Housefly Ant Mosquito Butterfly

Homes of animals

Land animals

Animals that live on land are called land animals like cows, horses, elephants and lions.

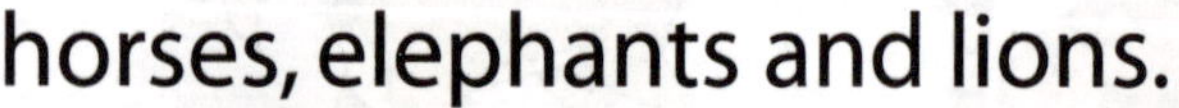

Lion

Elephant

Horse

Water animals

Animals that live in water are called water animals like fish, sharks and octopus.

Fish Octopus

Amphibians

Animals that live in water and land both are called amphibians like frogs, crocodiles and tortoises.

Arboreal

Animals like monkey, birds and some insects live on trees. These are called arboreal animals.

A. Fill in the blanks to complete the sentences with the given words.

Rhinoceros, Wings, Emu, Frog, Cat

1. ______________ is a big animal.
2. Birds have ______________ to fly.
3. ______________ is a bird but cannot fly.
4. ______________ lives on land.
5. ______________ can live both on land and in water.

B. Match the pictures with the correct options.

has wings

big animal

insect

lives on tree

C. Match the following.

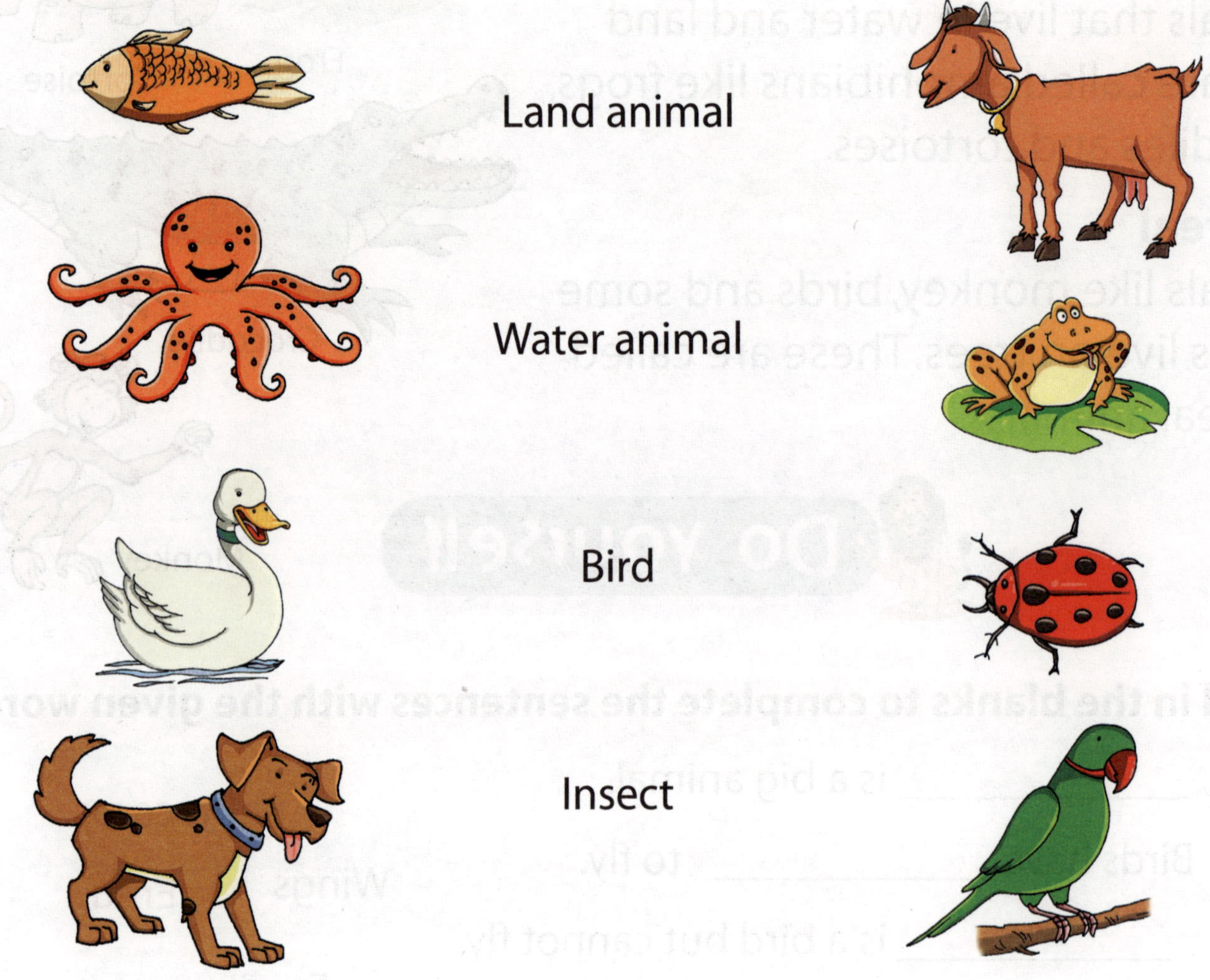

D. Answer the following questions.

1. Write the names of two animals that live on land.

   ____________ ____________

2. Write the names of two animals that live in the jungle.

   ____________ ____________

3. Write the names of an animal that can live on land as well as in water.

   ____

E. Find the names of animals hidden in the word search puzzle with the help of the picture clues.

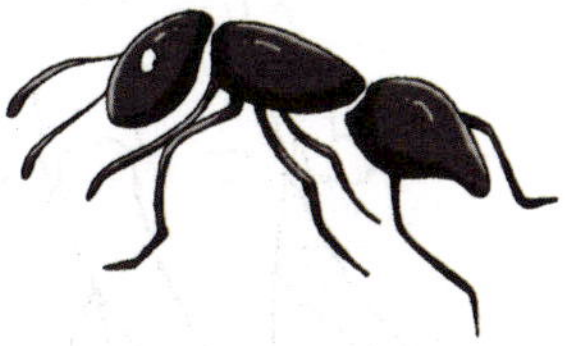

C	R	O	W	E	W	X	D	H	G	L
R	I	S	Q	U	I	R	R	E	L	A
A	N	T	C	G	U	W	D	L	I	G
T	I	G	E	R	Q	E	W	C	O	W
S	L	P	T	D	V	S	U	K	N	L
A	S	D	M	O	N	K	E	Y	Z	Z
O	S	T	R	I	T	C	H	J	K	L

F. Join the dots and see what animal you get. Do not forget to colour it.

Activity time

Paste the pictures of two of each— land animals, water animals, amphibians in your scrapbook and write their names.

11 Food and Shelter of Animals

Food of animals

Animals need food to live and grow like us. Different animals eat different kinds of food.

Some animals eat **plants** like cows, goats, elephants and giraffes.

Cow

Goat

Elephant

Giraffes

Some animals eat **flesh of other animals** like tigers, lions and wolves.

Lion

Wolf

Tiger

Some animals eat **grains** like rats, hens and squirrels.

Hen Rat Squirrel

Some animals eat **insects and worms** like lizards, frogs, spiders and bats.

Spider Frog Lizard Bat

Some animals eat both **plants and the flesh of other animals** like crows, cats and bears.

Crow Cat Bear

Homes of animals

Animals need homes like us to live in. Different animals live in different types of homes. Home protects them from heat, cold, rain and enemies.

Some animals make their homes on their own.

A bird makes a nest. A bee makes a hive. A spider makes a web. A rabbit makes a burrow.

Some animals find their homes in the jungle on their own.

A lion lives in a den.

A monkey lives on trees.

Some animals live in a home made by man.

A dog lives in a kennel.

A horse lives in a stable.

A hen lives in a coop.

A cow lives in a shed.

A. Tick the correct picture.

1.   eat grains.
2.   makes nest.
3.   lives in a kennel.
4.   lives in a stable.

B. Fill in the blanks with the correct option.

1. Animals need ____________ to live and grow. (food/cloth)
2. Hens eat ____________. (grass/grains)
3. A lion lives in a ____________. (den/hole)
4. A rabbit lives in a ____________. (nest/burrow)
5. An elephant eats ____________. (plants/animals)
6. Birds make ____________. (nest/web)

C. Answer the following questions in your own words.

1. Why do animals need food?

   ____

2. Name any two animals that eat plants.

   ____________________ ____________________

3. Name any two animals that eat insects.

   ____________________ ____________________

4. What do animals like tiger and lion eat?

   ____

5. Why do animals need home?

   ____

D. **The names of the homes of some animals are given below. Unjumble the words and write there names.**

	Animal	Shelter
1. ATSLEB	__________	__________
2. END	__________	__________
3. TENS	__________	__________
4. EIHV	__________	__________
5. RUBRWO	__________	__________

E. **Help the lioness go back to her den.**

Activity time

Visit a zoo along with your parents. Make a list of all the animals you see. Paste their pictures in your scrapbook and write about the food they eat.

UNIT 4 Human Body

12 Our Body

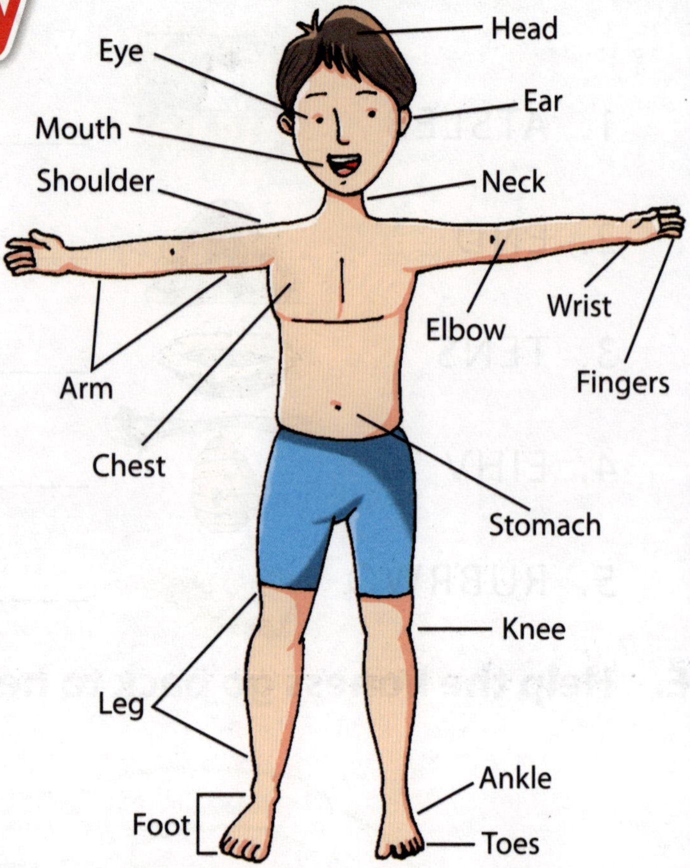
Head
Eye
Ear
Mouth
Shoulder
Neck
Wrist
Elbow
Fingers
Arm
Chest
Stomach
Knee
Leg
Ankle
Foot
Toes

Our body has many parts. All the parts are important. Each part has a different function. Our legs help us to walk, run and play. Our hands help us to hold things, to write and to clap.

Walk

Play

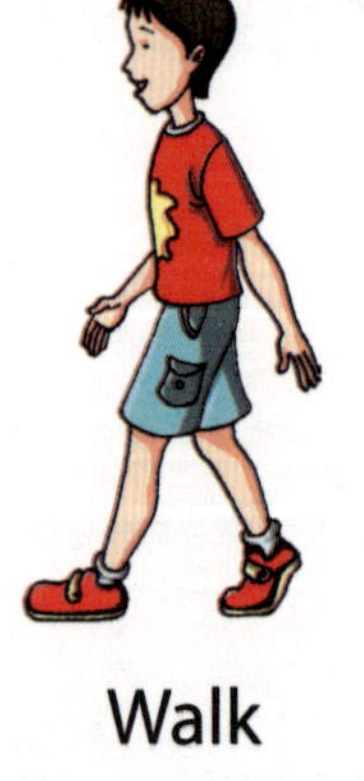

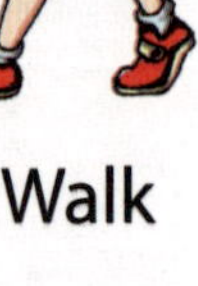

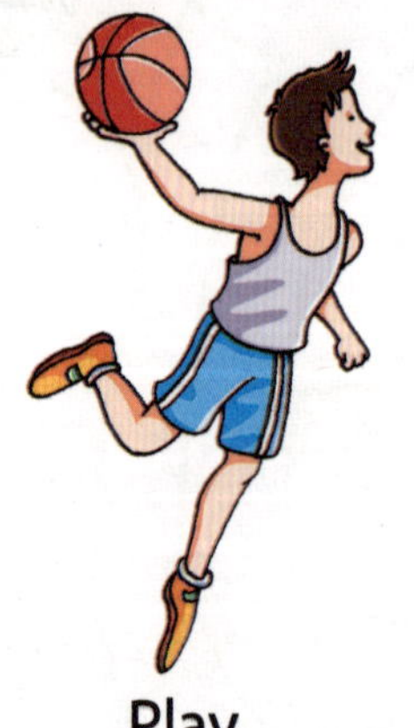

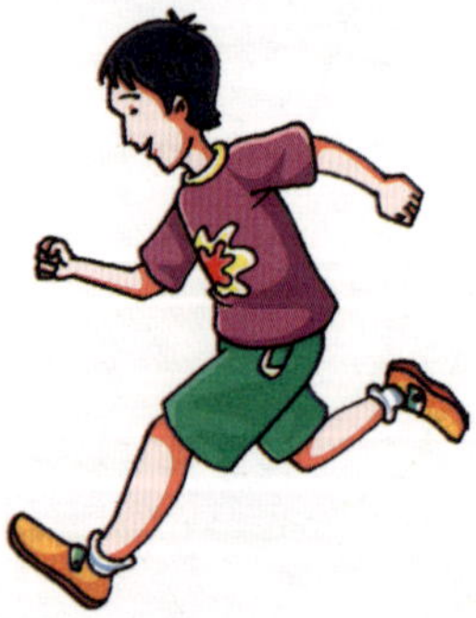

Run

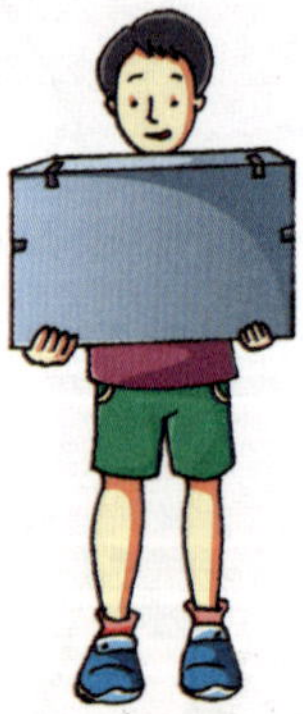

Hold

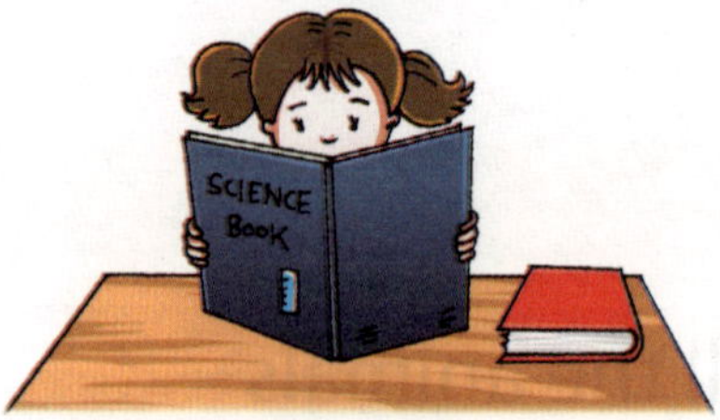
SCIENCE
Book

Read

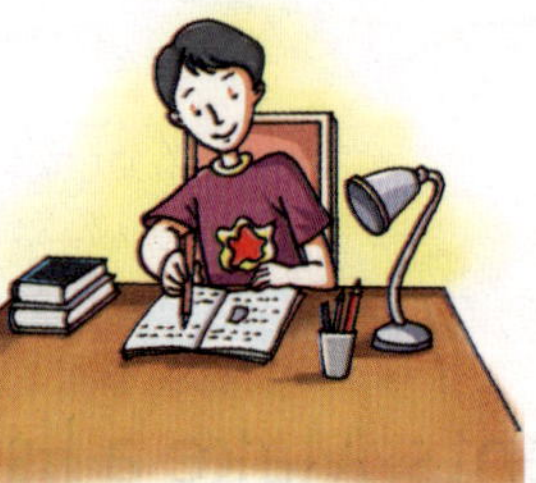

Write

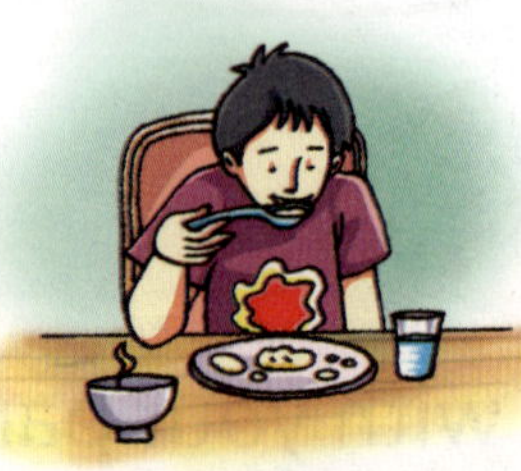

Eat

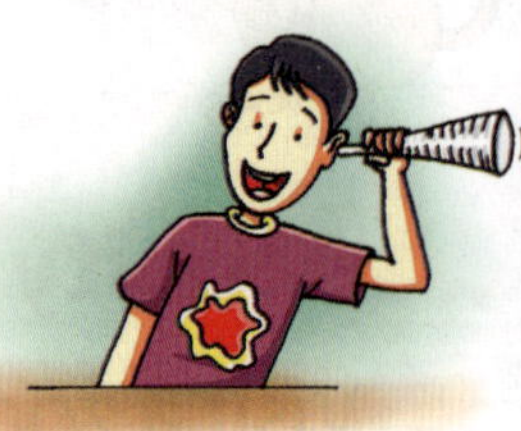

Hear

Eyes help us to **see** things.

Nose helps us to **smell**.

Ears help us to **hear**.

Tongue helps us to **taste**.

Skin helps us to **feel**.

The eyes, ears, nose, tongue and skin are together called **sense organs**. These organs are our friends. They help us to know the world around us.

Do yourself

A. The names of a few parts of our body are given below. Write how many you have for each part in the boxes given.

Hands		Nose		Fingers	
Eyes		Legs		Feet	
Toes		Arms		Ears	

B. Tell us something more about yourself.

1. I like to ________________. (dance / sing / play)
2. My hair is ______________. (straight / curly)
3. I like ____________________ things. (sweet / salty)
3. My teeth are ______________ in colour. (white / yellow)
4. I have _________________ cheeks. (yellow / pink)

C. Match the following activities with the part of the body.

A	**B**
Reading book	
Holding things	
Walking	
Smelling	

D. Unjumble the names of the given parts of the body.

1. AHDN ___________
2. RMA ___________
3. OSNE ___________
4. KENC ___________

E. In the space given below draw any two parts of our body and colour it.

Activity time

Paste five pictures of various actions done by people or animals in your scrapbook. Do write which part of the body is used to do the action.

13 Our Food

Can you tell me what do you like to eat the most? Is it ice cream, candies or fruit salad? We all eat and drink many things during the day. All these things are called food.

We need food to live and grow. It makes us healthy and strong. Food gives us energy to do our work. We eat different types of food like fruits, vegetables, pulses and cereals. We drink water, milk and juices too.

Sources of food

Plants and animals are the sources of our food. We get fruits, vegetables, cereals and pulses from plants.

Vegetables

Pulses

Fruits

We get milk, eggs, meat and fish from animals.

Fish

Eggs

Chicken

How to be healthy

- We should eat fresh fruits and vegetables.
- We should wash fruits and vegetables before eating.
- We should drink milk everyday. Milk makes our bones and teeth strong.
- We should not overeat.
- We should not waste food.
- We should not eat dirty or unhealthy food.
- We should not eat lot of chips, chocolates, candies and cold drinks. These are junk food. These make us unhealthy.
- We should always eat clean and healthy food.

A. Write (F) for fruit and (V) for vegetable for the given pictures.

B. Answer the following questions.

1. Why do we need food?

____

____

2. What are the sources of food?

____

____

3. From where do we get milk?

____

____

4. Write any two things we get from plants.

____

____

5. Why should we not eat dirty food?

____

____

C. Choose the correct word from the fruit basket and fill in the blanks.

1. _______________ makes us healthy and strong.
2. We get fruits and vegetables from _______________.
3. Milk makes our bones and teeth _______________.
4. We should not eat lot of _______________.
5. We get eggs from _______________.

animals
candies
plants
food
strong

D. Put a tick (✓) for correct statements and a (X) for a wrong statement.

1. Healthy food makes us strong. ☐
2. We should overeat. ☐
3. We should not waste food. ☐
4. We should eat lot of chips and candies. ☐
5. We should eat fresh and clean fruits and vegetables. ☐

E. Who am I?

1. I am brown in colour. Children love my chips! ______________
2. I am purple. I have a crown on my head. ______________.
3. I am yellow and sweet. I am the king of fruits.

   ____

4. I am not a lady, and I look like a finger. ______________

Activity time

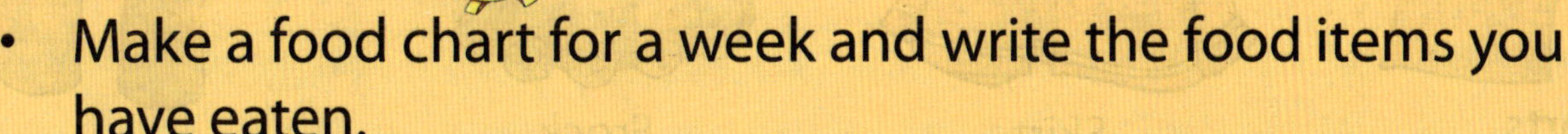

- Make a food chart for a week and write the food items you have eaten.

	Sun	Mon	Tue	Wed	Thurs	Fri	Sat
Breakfast							
Lunch							
Dinner							

- Draw the pictures of your favourite fruits and vegetables (any three) in your notebooks.

14 Our Clothes

We wear clothes to cover our body. Clothes save us from heat, cold, wind and rain.

Types of clothes

We wear different clothes at different times of the year according to the seasons. We should always wear clean clothes.

Cotton clothes

We wear cotton clothes in summer. They keep our bodies cool.

Cotton clothes are made up of cotton. We get cotton from cotton plants.

Shorts

Skirt

Frock

Coat & Trousers

Woollen clothes

We wear woollen clothes in winter. They keep our bodies warm. Woollen clothes are made up of wool.
We get wool from sheep.

Woollen Cap

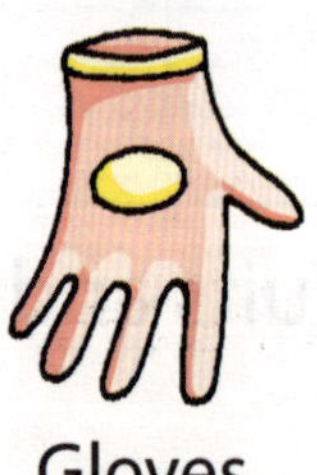

Gloves

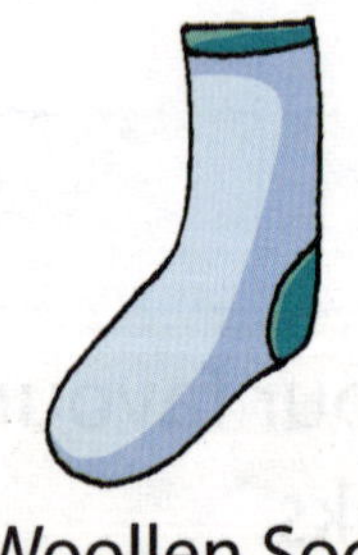

Woollen Socks

Sweater

Clothes for monsoon

We wear raincoats in the rainy season or monsoon. It protects us from rain. We also use umbrellas and gumboots.

Gumboots

Umbrellas

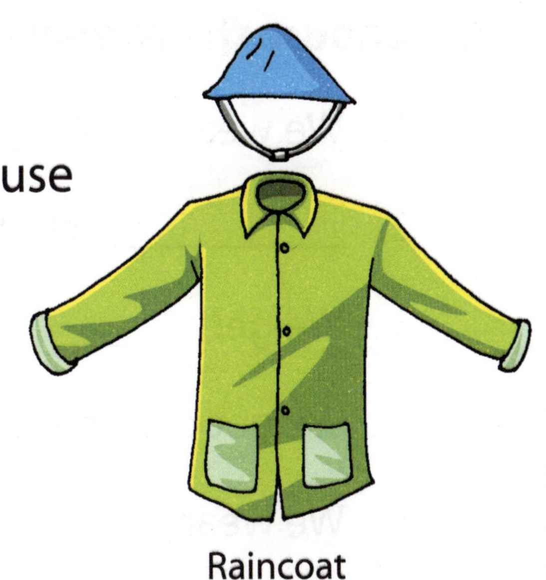
Raincoat

Do Yourself

A. Divij is feeling very hot today. Suggest him the types of clothes he should wear to beat the heat.

______________________________.

B. Richa is wearing woollen clothes. Complete the name of the clothes she is wearing.

1. S ____ E ____ T ____ R
2. ____ ____ P
3. GL ____ V ____ S

C. Choose the correct option and fill in the blanks.

1. We wear ____________ clothes in summer. (cotton / woollen)
2. ____________ clothes keep us warm in winter. (cotton / woollen)
3. We get ____________ from sheep. (cotton / wool)
4. We get cotton from ____________. (sheep / plant)
5. We wear ____________ to protect ourselves from rain. (raincoat / swimming suit)
6. Cotton clothes keep our bodies ____________. (hot / cool)

D. Match the clothes with their names.

A	B
Frock	
Dungaree	
Coat	
Jeans	
Top and Skirt	

E. Look at the given pictures and write their names in the correct columns given below.

Summer season	Winter season	Rainy season

F. Answer the questions given below.

1. Why do we need to wear clothes?

   ____

2. What type of clothes should we wear in summer?

   ____

3. When do we wear woollen clothes?

   ____

Activity time

- Paste a little cotton and a hand-made paper in your scrapbook and find out which one is rough and which is smooth.
- Colour the given picture.

15 Good Habits

Good habits keep us healthy and fit. We must practice good habits in our daily lives.

Keeping clean

1. Brush your teeth twice a day—morning and night.
2. Take a bath with soap everyday and use a clean towel to wipe yourself.
3. Wear clean clothes and comb your hair.
4. Wash your hands before and after eating.
5. Trim your nails regularly.
6. Keep your eyes, ears and nose clean.

Keeping fit

1. Wake up early every morning.
2. Go to bed early every night.
3. Try to do some exercise daily. It will make your body healthy and strong.
4. Try to play outdoors. Playing games, running and swimming are good for health.
5. Take proper rest. A good sleep makes us feel fresh and full of energy.

A few more things

1. Always sit, walk and stand straight.
2. Use your hanky while sneezing or coughing.
3. Do not bite your nails.
4. Eat from your own plate.
5. Drink from your own glass.
6. Do not write on the walls of your home or school.
7. Do not spit on the floor or on the road.
8. Use a dustbin to throw the waste.
9. Keep your things at a proper place.
10. Do not quarrel with others.
11. Do not waste water and electricity. Turn off the tap and also the switches when not in use.
12. Learn to recycle things especially paper.

A. Fill in the blanks with the right word.

early	straight	clean	combed	bent	dirty
late	uncombed	bag	dustbin	hanky	

1. Wake up __________ in the morning.
2. Use your __________ while sneezing or coughing.
3. Use __________ to throw the waste.
4. Keep your hair __________.
5. Wear __________ clothes everyday.
6. Always sit, walk and stand __________.

B. Look at the pictures given below. Write the number in the box indicating the correct order of these activities.

C. Answer the questions in your own words.

1. Why should we exercise daily?

   ____

2. Why must we brush our teeth?

   ____

3. What must we do before and after eating?

   ____

4. Write any four good habits to stay healthy.

   ____

D. Match the given good habits with the things you need to do them.

1. Trimming nails

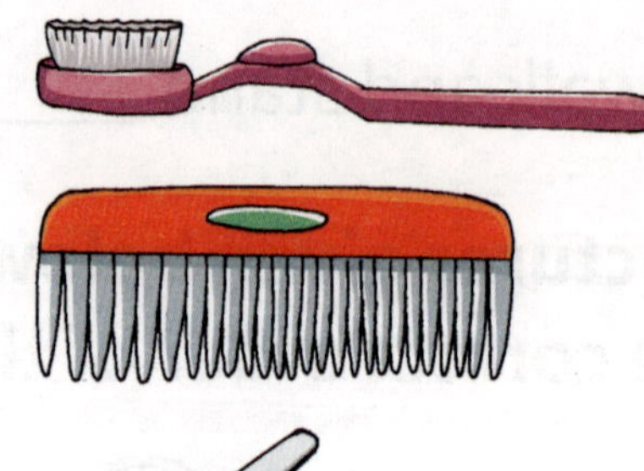

2. Coughing and sneezing

3. Brushing teeth

4. Combing hair

5. Throwing waste

Activity time

- Make a poster on five good habits which you think are most important.
- The given table contains some good habits that we should practice everyday. After a week, tick (✓) those habits which you have done and cross (X) if you have not practiced a good habit on a particular day.

	Activity to be done every day	**Mon**	**Tue**	**Wed**	**Thurs**	**Fri**	**Sat**	**Sun**
1.	Wake up early in the morning							
2.	Brush your teeth twice a day							
3.	Exercise daily							
4.	Take a bath everyday							
5.	Wash hands before and after eating							

Activity time

- Alice and Elina are two friends. Here is a picture showing the rooms of both these friends. Look at the pictures and colour the tidy room.

Alice's room

Elina's room

UNIT 5 Universe

16 Air

Air is very important for all living things. There is no life without air. All living things need air to breathe. Air is all around us.

We cannot see air, we cannot touch air but we can feel it.

Moving air is called **wind**. It makes things move. Wind helps us in many ways:

1. Wind helps a **kite fly**.
2. It moves the **clouds** in the sky.
3. It helps a **boat sail**.

4. It helps the wet **clothes to dry**.
5. It helps a **parachute move** in sky.
6. It helps to turn **windmill**.

Drying Clothes

Parachute

Windmill

7. It helps a **glider fly**.
8. It helps to **light a fire**.
9. All living beings need **air to breathe**.
10. We need air to **fill balloons** and **tyres**.

Glider

A gentle wind is called **breeze**.

A strong and fast wind is called **storm**. A storm can be harmful. It can damage trees, houses and buildings. It can blow things away too!

A. Answer the following question.

1. What is wind?

   ____

2. Write any three uses of air.

   ____

3. What is breeze?

   ____

4. How is storm harmful?

   ____

B. Match the following

1. A wind helps boat to	air
2. A storm can be	move
3. Moving air is called	sail
4. All living beings need	harmful
5. Air makes things	wind

C. Look at the pictures and write the first letter of their names in the blanks and see what new words you get.

________ ________ ________ ________

__________ __________ __________ __________ __________

D. List the things that will be moved by air.

1. ________________ 2. ________________

3. ________________ 4. ________________

5. ______________ 6. ______________

7. ______________ 8. ______________

E. The name of some things that move with the help of wind is given here. Unjumble the name and match with the pictures.

I N W M D L L I ______________

I E K T ______________

A S L I O A B T ______________

A P C R A U H E T ______________

Activity time

Take a candle. Ask your parent to light it. Cover the burning candle with a gas jar. See what happens. (Note: Perform this activity in the presence of parents or your teacher.)

17 Water

Water is very important for us. All living things need water. People, animals and plants cannot live without water. Water has many uses.

Uses of water

Water is used for **drinking**.

We use water for **cooking**.

We use water for **washing clothes**.

Water is used for **bathing**.

For Drinking

Cooking

Washing

Bathing

We use water for **cleaning**.

We use water for **watering plants**.

Water is also used for **putting out fire**.

Cleaning

Watering

Putting out fire

Sources of water

We get water from many sources like rain, river, pond, hand pump, wells and taps.

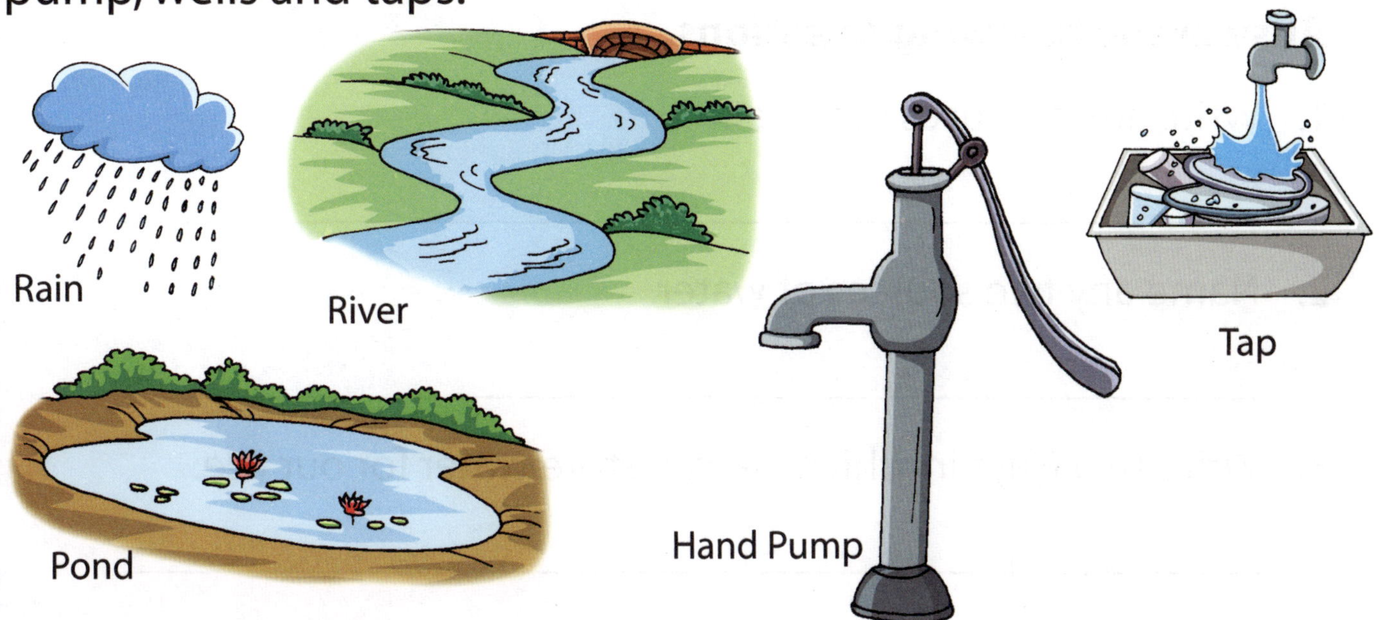

Storage of water

Water can be stored in many ways for example in dams, wells, tanks and buckets.

Water is precious. We must save water. We must not waste it. We must not throw waste into **water bodies**. We should always keep them clean.

A. Answer the following questions.

1. Write any two uses of water.

____

2. Name any two sources of water.

____

3. Write two ways in which we can store water for our use.

____

B. Put a cross (X) in the box given beside the picture showing wastage of water.

☐ ☐ ☐

C. Write (T) for the statements which are true and (F) for the ones that are false.

1. Plants can live without water. ☐
2. We must drink clean and pure water. ☐
3. Rain is the only source of water. ☐
4. We can throw waste in rivers. ☐
5. Water is used to put off fire. ☐

D. Sunny is going to the lake. But he has forgotten his way. Help him find his way to the lake.

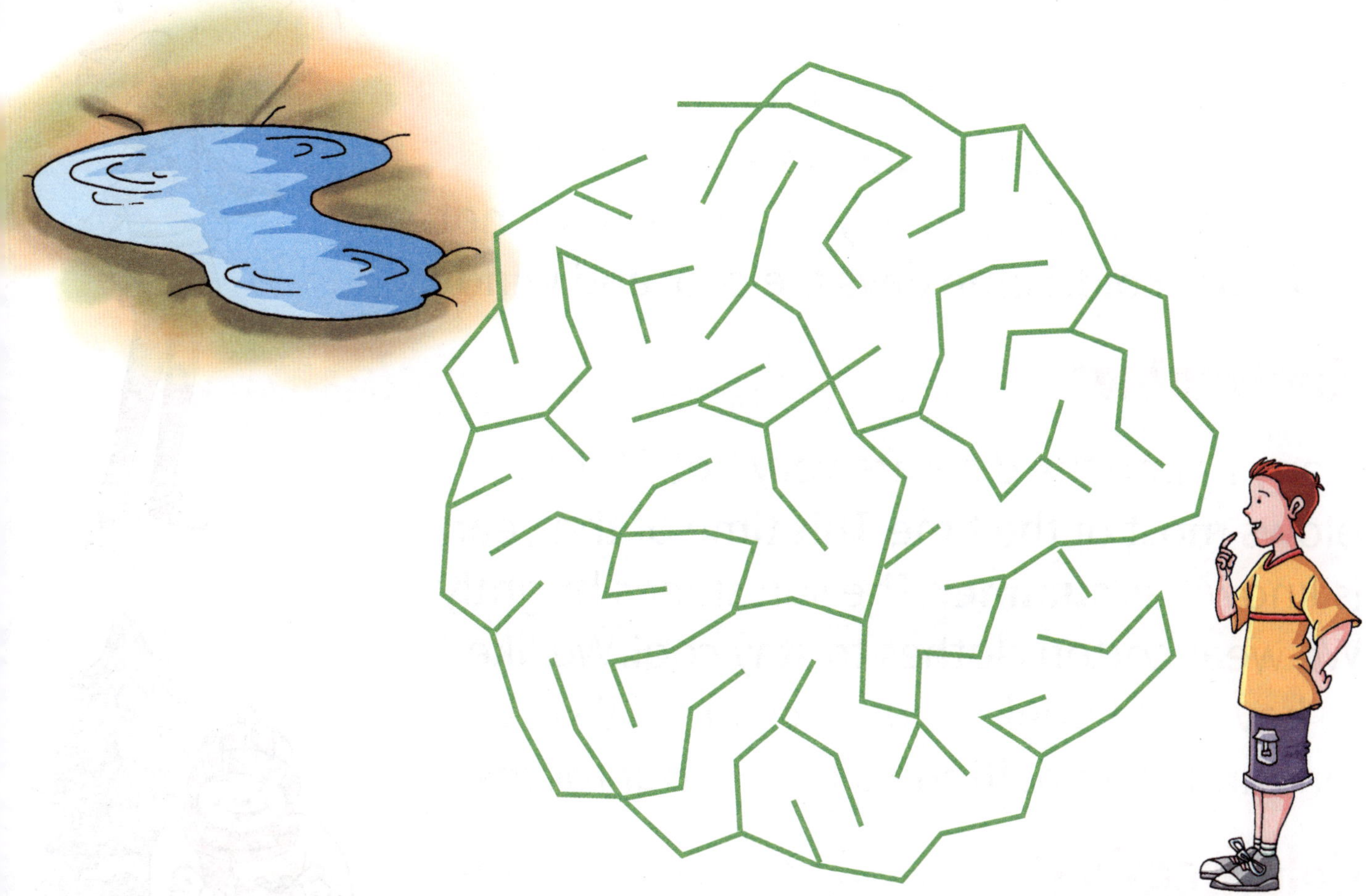

Activity time

- Paste pictures showing various uses of water in your scrapbook.
- Divide the class into three groups. Each group will make a poster on any one of the given topics.
  a. Uses of water
  b. Source of water
  c. Activities showing wastage of water

18 Weather

Weather is the condition of the air, sun, rain and clouds at a particular time. It keeps on changing from day to day. Some days are hot, some are cold. Some days are cool and windy.

Hot weather

Many a time the days are very hot. Hot air blows most of the time. This time of the year is known as **summer**. The sun shines brightly. We wear cotton clothes to stay cool. We like to have cold drinks and ice creams. We use fans and air conditioners to cool our rooms.

Cold weather

Sometimes the days and nights are very cold. Cold air blows and snow falls in some places. This time of the year is known as **winter**. We wear woollen clothes to stay warm. We have hot drinks like tea and coffee. We use room heaters.

Rainy weather

At one time of the year it rains a lot. This time of year is known as **monsoon**. Sometimes it rains for many days. We see a rainbow in the sky too. At this time, we use umbrellas, raincoats and gumboots to keep ourselves dry.

Windy weather

On some days the wind blows strongly. Such days are said to have a **windy weather**. Sometimes wind blows so strongly that it uproots trees and harms the buildings also.

We have some more types of weather like:

Cloudy weather

Foggy weather

Snowy weather

Pleasant weather

A. Fill in the blanks with the correct word.

Raincoat

Cotton

Tea

Paper boats

1. We wear __________ clothes in hot weather to stay cool.
2. We like to drink __________ in the cold weather.
3. We use __________ to protect ourselves from rain.
4. We play with __________ on a rainy day.

B. Answer the given questions.

1. What is weather?

____

2. What type of clothes do we wear in the cold weather?

____

3. What do we like to drink in the hot weather?

____

4. What do we sometimes see in the sky after a shower of rain?

____

C. Find the words in the word search which are given in the water drops.

Cold Hot Rain Windy Summer Winter Cotton

A	S	U	M	M	E	R
Z	L	C	V	P	W	A
X	C	O	L	D	I	I
H	O	T	H	Q	N	N
M	N	T	D	K	T	W
S	E	O	B	J	E	C
W	I	N	D	Y	R	X

19 In the Sky

The vast space we see above us is called the **sky**. We see the sun and clouds in the day time. We see the moon and the stars at night.

The sun

The sun shines brightly during the day. The day starts with the sunrise and ends with the sunset.

The sun rises in the east and sets in the west. It is a hot ball of fire. It is very big. It appears small because it is very far from us. The sun gives us heat and light. People, animals and plants need the sun to live.

The moon

We see moon at night. It looks like a big, silvery, round ball. But it is smaller than the sun. It gives us light at night. The moon changes its shape every night. Sometimes we see only a part of it or no moon at all.

The stars

We see lots of stars at night. Stars are actually very big in size. They look small because they are very far from us. Some stars form beautiful patterns in the sky.

Clouds

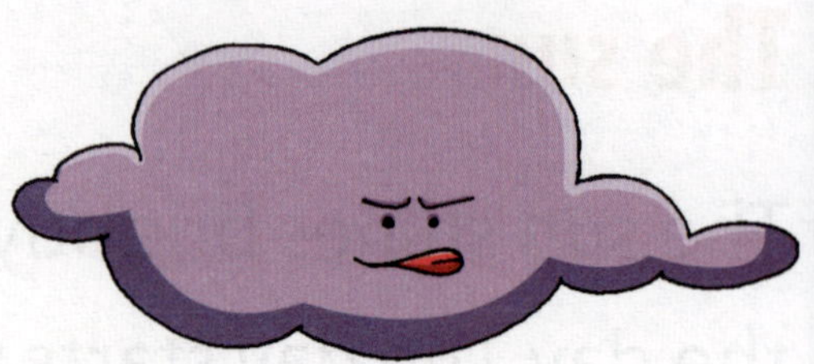

Sometimes we see clouds in the sky. Clouds are dark grey or white in colour. Dark clouds bring rain. Clouds float in the sky like balls of cotton wool.

A. Fill in the blanks with the correct word from the clouds.

1. The sun rises in the ______________ every morning.
2. The moon changes ______________ everyday.
3. There are a large number of ______________ in the sky.
4. ______________ bring rain.

B. Answer the questions given below.

1. When does a day change into night?

 ____

2. When do we see the moon?

 ____

3. Why do the stars look small?

 ____

4. Name the things we see in the daytime in the sky.

 ____

C. Look at the pictures below and unjumble the given words.

1. ONOM ________________
2. RTASS ________________
3. AINOWRB ________________
4. UNSIESR ________________

D. Who am I?

1. I give you heat and light in the day time.

____

2. We are many in number. We cover the sky at night.

____

3. I come at night and change my shape everyday.

____

4. I bring rain for you.

____

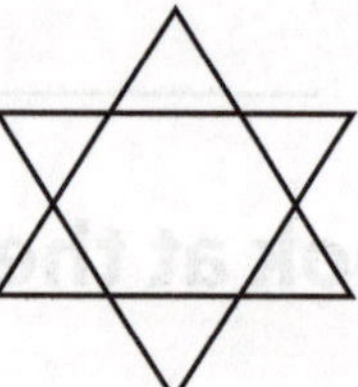

5. Count the number of triangles in the given star.

____

Activity time

- Draw the sun, the moon and the stars in your scrapbook. Colour and decorate the picture.
- Draw the shape of the moon and a star on a cardboard. Cut the shapes and stick silver paper on them. Now make a hole in each and hang them in your room.

TEST PAPER 1

A. Colour the box green for the true statement.

1. Living things cannot breathe. ☐
2. Non-living things can eat. ☐
3. A pen is a living thing. ☐
4. We take rest in the bedroom. ☐
5. We should not play with switches and plugs. ☐
6. We can take our hands out of a moving vehicle. ☐

B. Match the following

A	B
Mountain	stitches clothes for us
Tailor	is non-living thing
Mango	treats patients
Doctor	holds the plant upright
Stem	is a pulse
Gram	is a fruit

C. Draw the picture of your favourite fruit or vegetable.

D. Colour the living things red and non-living things green.

E. Answer the following questions.

1. Why do we need a house?

 ____

2. Write down any two things that a living thing can do?

 ____

3. Write any two safety rules that should be followed while playing.

 ____

4. Name the helper who sells medicine.

 ____

5. Write the function of a root in a plant.

 ____

F. Choose the correct answer and fill the blanks.

1. Non-living things __________ grow. (can/cannot)
2. We should keep our house __________. (tidy/untidy)
3. __________ lean out of a moving bus. (do/do not)
4. A __________ repairs water taps. (plumber/cobbler)
5. __________ prepare food for the plants. (leaf/root)

TEST PAPER 2

A. Look at the pictures carefully and write their names in the correct box.

B. Fill in the blanks with the correct word from the bracket.

1. We get fruits and vegetables from ____________ (plant/animals)
2. We should eat ____________ food. (healthy/unhealthy)
3. We wear ____________ when it rains. (sweater/raincoat)
4. We should go to bed ____________ at night. (early/late)

C. **Match the animals with their homes.**

Dog	coop
Lion	nest
Hen	kennel
Bird	den
Horse	stable

D. **Christie is doing a few activities. Tick the correct organ that she will use in doing the activity.**

1. Christie reads a book

a. Eyes ☐ b. Nose ☐ c. Neck ☐

2. Christie eats her dinner

a. Muscles ☐ b. Bones ☐ c. Mouth ☐

3. Christie smells a flower

a. Hair ☐ b. Fingers ☐ c. Nose ☐

4. Christie licks an ice cream

a. Eyes ☐ b. Legs ☐ c. Tongue ☐

TEST PAPER 3

A. Circle the activities that air can do.

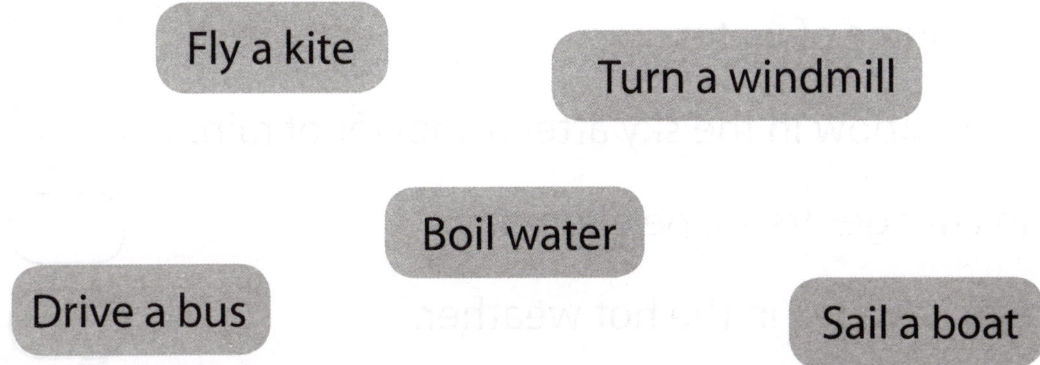

B. Write down the uses of water in the blanks given.

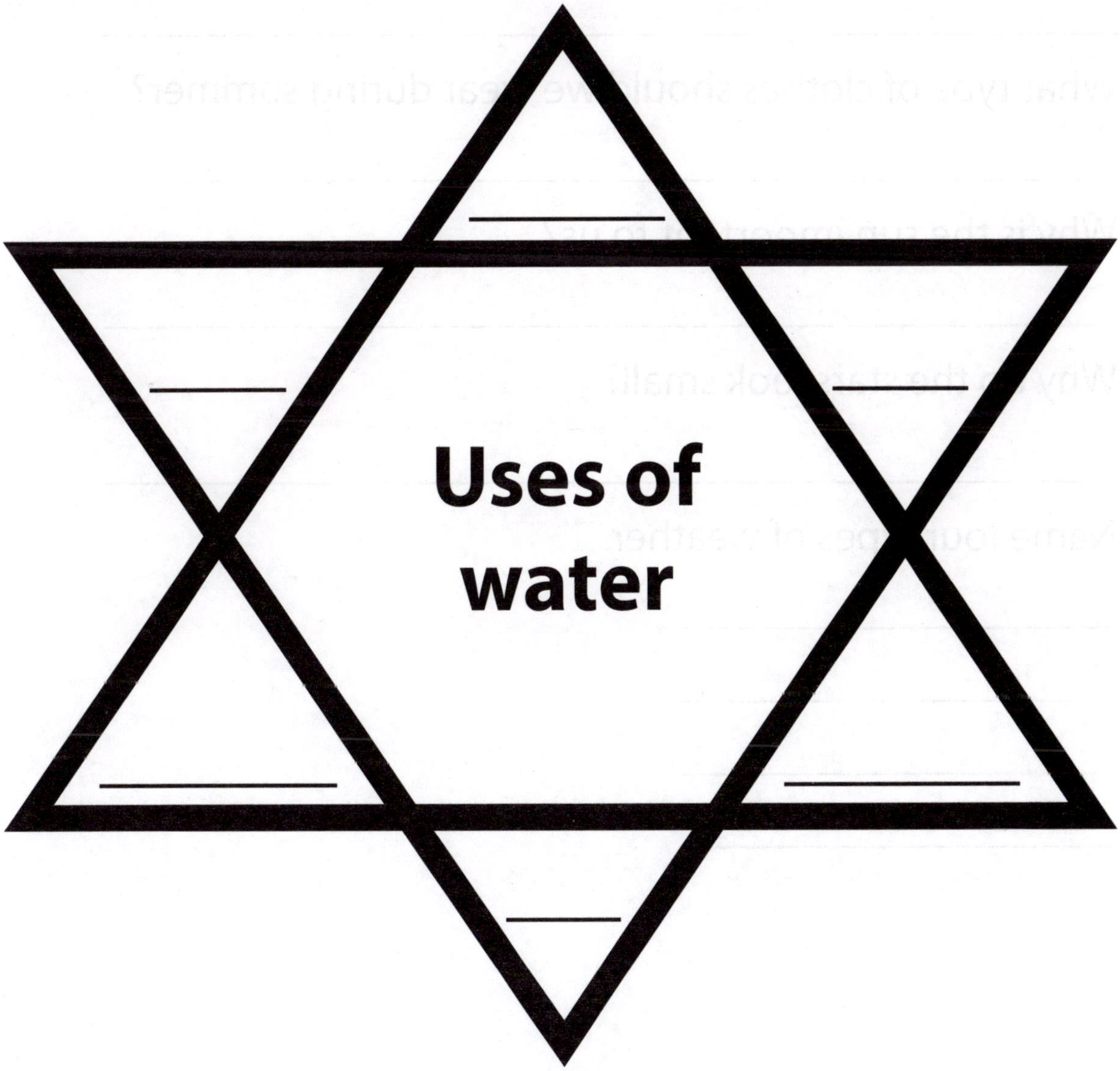

Uses of water

______

______

______

______

______

______

C. Write T for statements which are true and F for statements which are false.

1. A gentle wind is called storm. ◯
2. River is a source of water. ◯
3. We see a rainbow in the sky after a shower of rain. ◯
4. The Sun changes its shape everyday. ◯
5. We like to have tea in the hot weather. ◯

D. Answer the following questions.

1. What is strong and fast wind called?

   ____

2. What type of clothes should we wear during summer?

   ____

3. Why is the sun important to us?

   ____

4. Why do the stars look small?

   ____

5. Name four types of weather.

   ____

   ____

   ____

   ____